C000228651

Merry Xmas Stephan!
Have a happy '95 —
you deserve it c'os you're
such a wee star!
all my love,
Pamali

'in *soccer*
wonderland'

'in *soccer*
wonderland'

julian germain

Acknowledgements

Gill Smith. None of this would have been possible without her support, encouragement, vision and patience.

Andy Altmann and David Ellis. Designers of this book and my colleagues at Why Not Publishing.

Michael Whiteley. I am especially grateful for his collaboration on a number of interviews, for his assistance in photographing the children and myself, for the hours of discussion about football and for many good laughs.

Topham Picture Source. Thank you Alan Smith.

Michael Collins for his support, editorial advice and encouragement.

Mike Parsons for additional studio photography.

Paul Kirton of Sports and General.

'In Soccer Wonderland' received assistance from the Photographer's Gallery, London, Impressions Gallery, York, Subbuteo, Arkwright Clothing and the Football Association.

I would like to pay tribute to the many people connected with the following football clubs who kindly agreed to be questioned and photographed and who generously lent snapshots and keepsakes: Torrington, Corinthian, Consett, Blyth Spartans, Billericay Town, Tamworth, Bromsgrove Rovers, Huddersfield Town, Hayes, Crawley Town, Sunderland, Ipswich Town, Portsmouth, Doncaster Belles, Southampton Red Star, Cramlington Juniors, Whitley Bay Boys Club, Barnsley, Margate, Newcastle United and London Girls.

The staff and pupils at Wombwell School and Priory School, Barnsley and Rookhope Primary School, Co Durham.

Bret Rogers of the British Council, London and Mike Winters of the British Council, São Paulo.

Thanks also to: Suzie Joel, Sue Withers, Andrew Moller, Emma Parsons, David Lee, Paul Atkinson, David Chandler, Paul Wombell, Lorry Eason, Trevor Spencer, Ron Ellis, Keith Mason, John Gordon, Martin Herron, Peter Harvey, Kevin Ealand, Hedley, Andrea and Matthew Fairweather, Marcelo Rudini, Patricia Azevedo, Dean Walton, Ray Crawford, Ron Billings, Jeffery Jessop, the Emerson family, Roger Osborne, Mr L. Dewson, Bob Stockley, Gordon Wallis and John Daniels of Soccer Nostalgia, Dr Hugh Simons, the Hall family, Mr and Mrs Whiteley, Tommy Harris, Lee Allchorn, Vera Hutchinson, Fletch, Caroline Cole, Alan Outram, Graham Jones, Alan Smith, Helen Radcliffe, Vicky Hayward, Robert Chessyre, Edward Booth-Clibborn, Dave Willis, Huw Davies, Arabella Plouviez, the staff and students of the University of Sunderland, Colin Thompson Photography, Newcastle.

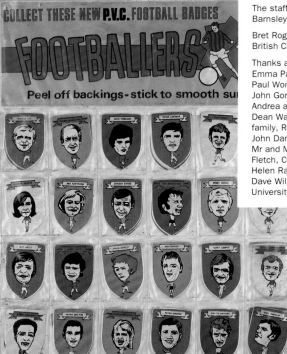

Book designed by Why Not Associates

Published by Booth-Clibborn Editions 1994

Copyright © 1994 Julian Germain

Photos pp. 16-17, 32, 33, 36-37, 40, 41, 70, 74-75,
88, 89, 92, 94-95, 98-99, 100, 111, 124-125, 156,
157, 160, 161 © Topham Picture Source.

Photos pp. 19, 114-115, 128-129, 130, 139
© Sports and General.

Photos pp. 52, 53 © Placar.

Photo pp. 54-55 © Jornal da Tarde.

Photo pp. 11 © Aerofilms.

Photo pp. 103 © Tommy Harris.

Photos pp. 44, 61, 121 reproduced by kind permission
of Dave Kindred of the East Anglian Daily Times.

Family snapshots © the owners.

Photo of Bobby Charlton pp. 78, we have been unable
to trace the owner of the copyright.

Distributed by: Internos Books
12 Percy Street, London W1P 9FB

Distributed in France by: InterArt Paris
1 Rue de L'Est, 75020 Paris, France.

ISBN 1873968 302

Copyright © 1994 Booth-Clibborn Editions
All rights reserved.
No part of this publication may be reproduced,
stored in a retrieval system or in any form or by
any means – electronic, mechanical, photocopy,
recording or otherwise – without prior permission
of the copyright owners

Printed and bound in Hong Kong
Toppan Printing Co.

'in *soccer*
Wonderland'

for Richard and Tim

'in soccer wonderland'

julian germain

Glue here only

138
TOMMY CARROLL

IPSWICH TOWN

(A full biography on this
player will be found in the
appropriate space in the
album).

I was born on September 25th, 1962,

on the day Ipswich Town

beat Floriana of Malta 10 - 0 in the European Cup.

Their biggest ever win and all in all a good day.

I have always wanted to be a great footballer.

However, I'm now 31 years old and resigned to the fact that
I will never play for England, or for that matter Ipswich.

Instead, I find myself going next door to ask the neighbours if Paul, their 14-year-old, can come out to play. He can, after he's fed the chickens, so I go home and change into trainers, track suit bottoms and Ipswich's orange 'away' top, now obsolete. Thirty minutes later, dusk has arrived but Paul hasn't; if he doesn't bloody hurry up it'll be too dark. I'm about to do something useful with my life when, thankfully, the tell-tale thud of ball on concrete announces his arrival. We play on the primary school's miniature football pitch, the only bit of flat land in the village. There is light rain, wet grass, soft ground and mud. **Perfect.**

'Headers and crosses', 'Ballie against the wallie' and 'Three and in'; the same games I played with my brothers when we were growing up in Ipswich. Our house was on the ring road which meant we could claim, with a shred of justification, to live on the same street as Alf Ramsey - *the ENGLAND MANAGER*. The house rumoured to belong to the great man was more than a mile away (it was the white one with a caravan parked in the drive) and in 1970, aged seven and a half, I made the epic journey around Ipswich's version of the 'North Circular' to pop a carefully drafted request for autographs through his door. I didn't actually see him. In fact, despite years of looking, none of us ever even caught so much as a glimpse. But a few weeks after submitting my plea, I did receive the official England World Cup Squad autograph sheet through the post.

My destiny, to be an Ipswich fan, may have been sealed shortly afterwards when our new lounge carpet was laid by Tommy Carroll, the Town's right back and an Eire international. Georgie Best owned trendy boutiques and swanned around in an E-Type Jag but Tommy Carroll turned up in a knackered old van to lay our carpet. The following Sunday afternoon, sprawled on the very same carpet, *I watched him score a penalty* on 'Match of the Week'.

He was my hero.

He was a professional first division footballer.

~~He laid *our* carpet.~~

He was on the telly

and I*'d met him.*

Failing my 11- and 13-plus exams earned me a five-year sentence in a rugby playing school. In 1975 I missed the 6th round F.A. Cup tie against the then mighty Leeds United because of a rugby match in some far flung market town. I vividly recall the nail-biting and never-ending coach journey back. By the time I eventually got down to the ground, after a gut-busting two mile sprint, there were already 38,010 people inside, including both of my brothers, who had made it to the soccer-playing grammar school. The place was bursting at the seams. Ipswich's record attendance and me locked out because of rugby.

At home we played football: in the garden (after we'd cleared up the dog shit), on the landing with tightly scrunched and sellotaped newspaper, or in the lounge with a ping pong ball that was bounced off the wall and headed or volleyed towards the sofa, which was the goal. The keeper was able to dive spectacularly across the room without fear of serious injury.

We played Subbuteo in the hall downstairs by the front door because it had the smoothest patch of carpet in the house and you could crawl all the way round the pitch without some obstruction adversely affecting your balance while attempting to 'flick'. The pitch was ironed flat, the players lined up and the timer set for ten minutes, but, inevitably, at a crucial moment the doorbell would ring or a double glazing leaflet was shoved through the letter box, precipitating a frenzied pitch invasion by the dog. **I wonder why we never played on the table?**

football is nothing

romance and fantasy

But I have my moments of real-life glory. Even in a 40-minute kick about with Paul I might time it just right on the half volley and effortlessly, with my left foot, send a bullet of a shot smacking against the crossbar from 20 yards. Once, playing for Chelsea Casuals, a hopeless bunch of old codgers, I scored a hat-trick that I will treasure till the day I die. I could easily draw you a Boys Own Soccer Annual type diagram of each goal.

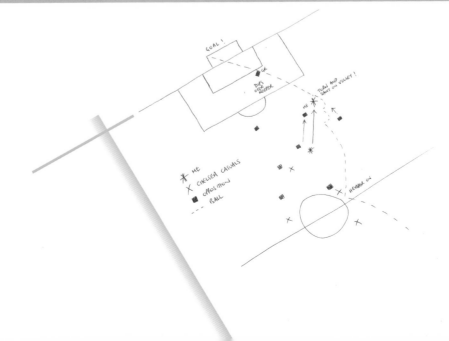

without

LIVERPOOL
Football Club

Admit

Photographer
(via Players' Entrance)

VERSUS .... IPSWICH.
Date .... 2·6·FEB 1992
Kick-off ....
This Portion to be Retained   General Secretary

'I'm saddened by all these guys in their posh suits, sitting in executive boxes.'

'I remember vividly my father telling me to prepare myself for this. The football was secondary to everything else that was going on. The walk to the ground with this enormous amount of people. There must have been fifty or sixty thousand. This was a very happy crowd.

The noise. The colour.

All these new experiences! I was very aware that if I lost sight of my father, it would probably be the last I ever saw of him. The people around us were very noisy, the stadium was very noisy.

I was

pretty

spellbound

by

the

whole

thing.'

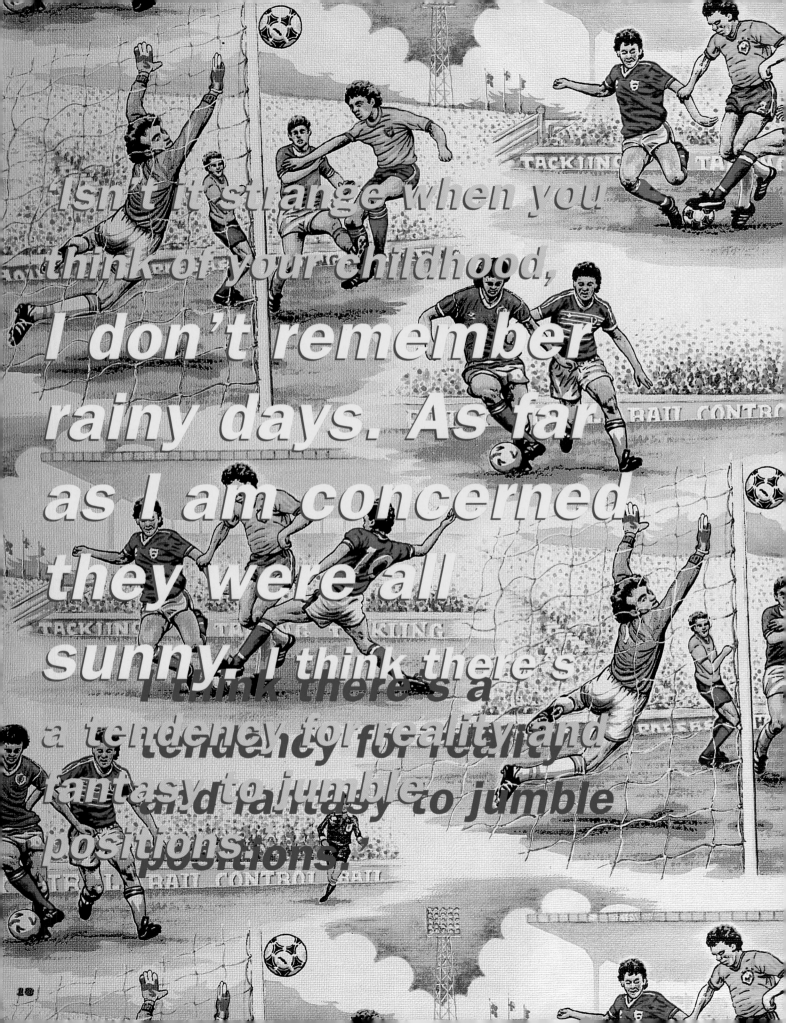

"Isn't it strange when you think of your childhood, I don't remember rainy days. As far as I am concerned they were all sunny. I think there's a tendency for reality and fantasy to jumble positions."

18

me *in soccer wonderland*

"Brian Talbot
about to
cross"

Subbuteo was invented
in 1947 by Peter Adolph
from Tunbridge Wells.

subbuteo

SUBBUTEO

*The game is played competitively in over 50
countries, including Nigeria and Paraguay.*

6th Round FA Cup

27th February 1932

Huddersfield Town 0

Arsenal 1

Record Attendance

67,037

The word Subbuteo is
derived from the Latin
name for the Hobby
Falcon - *Falco Subbuteo 
Subbuteo*

subbuteo

SUBBUTEO

I think about football all the time;
at home,
on the bus,
when I'm at school,
bored in a lesson,
wherever.

I just sit there and **dream** *about football.*

At night, I lie in bed and play my computer football game and then I go to sleep thinking about football, about me sticking the ball in the back of the net, scoring a brilliant goal and stuff like that.

32

When you do *a really brilliant header* you feel total joy.

You feel like, **YESSS !**

I did that and they all shout,

'Well done Melvin. Keep doing it.'

We always pretend it's a big match, you know, we're Man United and you're Leeds and we can all be whoever we want. Me mate Paul Brown is usually Mark Hughes and Davey Brook is Cantona. And you commentate as you play,

'Cantona's on the ball,

he takes one player,

takes another,

that's a dangerous looking cross,

Hughes is coming in...

beautiful header...

he's scorrrrrrrrrred...

GOOOAAALLLLL

...and the crowd are going wild!'

84

I was born Sunday February 20th, 1921. I shall be 74 this next February. A lot of people don't know which actual day of the week they were born on, you know, and if you give me the date I can usually work out which day of the week it was.

Okay, shall I try you out on my mum then? She was born on May 15th, 1939.

Just before the war, May 15th, 1939. Well that shouldn't take too long...erm...a Monday.

How on earth do you know that?

Well, Ipswich's last match that season in the league was May 6th at Bournemouth, and Monday was May 8th, when we played Aston Villa in the Hospital Cup. Therefore, the next Monday would be the 15th. We drew nil – nil at Bournemouth and Aston Villa beat us 3 – 2 in the Hospital Cup. Davies and Little got the Ipswich goals.

HAPPY BIRTHDAY 11

Go for 25th September, 1962, my birthday.

Well, that was a Tuesday, the day we played Floriana in the European Cup. Was that the first or the second leg? Yes, that would be the second leg. We won 10 – 0! Crawford got five, erm...Ellsworthy got one, that's six. Did Phillips get two? That's eight. Stephenson got one and Moran got one. That'd be ten. We had A.C. Milan in the next round, went there and lost three – nought and beat 'em here 2 – 1 in the second leg. That was a good game. We bombarded their goal and did just about everything but score.

I was always interested in football from when I went to school. I suppose that grow and grow with you. If you have anything to eat you like, that grow with you, don't it? I think football's the same. It just becomes part of you.

I went to school in Earl Soham, about 14 mile from Ipswich, nice little village, used to be a population of 500 in my day. When I went to school I used to play football a lot and I could score a few goals. Saturdays I used to go with the boys and we always played on the village green and then sometimes we'd go to a meadow. I weren't very old then but I followed the football through the paper. I was interested in Sheffield United because I had an uncle living there and he used to send me the Sheffield Green 'Un each week. Ipswich would've been in the Southern Amateur League then and I used to read all about them even though they were an amateur side.

One day the education committee sent round a letter to the headmaster and he read it out at morning assembly, about a football game at Portman Road between Suffolk and Arsenal. Arsenal were really great then! That was to commemorate 50 years of the Suffolk County Football Association. Well, the education committee had sent round permission that boys could go but they'd have to raise one and six pence. A shilling to go on the bus and six pence to go in the ground. Course, in those days that was a lot of money, a lot of 'em couldn't raise that very easily, they'd hardly got a shoe to the foot, big families you see. Anyway they scrounged the money up somewhere. I'd went and told my mother and she give me two shillings, so that was all right!

Anyhow, the bus was full and off we went. That was about a 25-seater, 1930 Dennis model. A nice bus in those days. RT8035 was the registration number. We left Earl Soham about half-past-one time, that'd take at least

an hour cos they haven't got the engines like they've got today and there was 14 miles to go. That was the first time I went to Portman Road, before there were any stands. That was all open there then. I remember standing behind the goal where Churchman's stand is now. That was a lovely sunny afternoon, couldn't have been better and both sides had their photographs taken just in front of that goal. They kicked-off at four o'clock. The Arsenal side was Bradshaw, Leslie Compton, Bacussi, Cartwright, Sidie and John. He was a Welsh international and the following Wednesday he was playing for Wales against Ireland. The right winger was Rogers, then Parkin, Cox, Holden and Denis Compton. Arsenal won 6 – 1. Wednesday March 20th, 1935. That was a memorable day, the first time I went to a big match. I was fourteen and a month exactly.

I well remember going to the match with Aston Villa in the F.A. Cup third round replay, Wednesday January 11th,1939.That was our first season in the Football League. We were in Division Three South and they were in the first division. It was a 2.15 kick-off and I was in there at 12.15. Record gate, stood for years, 28,194. You couldn't move! Couldn't fall down cos you couldn't move! That was packed in like sardines that day! I always used to go to the loo beforehand because if you came out you'd lose yer place! I saw all right though and that was a good match. Aston Villa won 2 – 1. They got the winner about two or three minutes from time. Mick Burns, the Ipswich goalkeeper, followed the referee right the way to the half-way line protesting about whether someone had hand-balled it, but the referee wouldn't give in. They don't when they give a decision do they? That was disappointing when we lost but that was a lovely bright sunny day, irrespective that it was January.

Ipswich was Alf Ramsey's first blood as manager. He come out the Spurs first team straight here in August 1955. We were Division Three South when he came. Well, we lost the first match at home to Torquay and then I don't think we lost another home game the rest of that season. We finished third in the league, just pipped for promotion.

In '56 – '57 we had seven defeats in the first nine matches, yet we come off and won it! Let me see... '56 – '57...Bailey, Carberry, Malcolm, Billy Baker, he was a Welsh international, Doug Rees, John Ellsworthy, Billy Reed, Doug Millward...erm... Tom Garneys, let me see now, Tom Carter wasn't...the number ten would be Phillips, oh LEADBETTER. And sometimes McLuckie and sometimes Miles. He died last week, Neil Miles, and he's being cremated on Tuesday. That was mostly the team. Then we had another four seasons before we won the second division title.

The first game in the first division was August19th, 1961. We went to Bolton Wanderers and drew nil – nil. Then we lost to Burnley and Manchester City. People were thinking, 'Oh, one point from a possible six.' But on March 31st, 1962, we beat the Wolves 3 – 2 at home and that took us to the top of the table. We were a point ahead of Burnley but they had a better goal average and four games in hand. They kept in the Cup, you see. They were getting a lot of games and when they played the league matches they kept losing. Our last match was on April 28th, 1962 against Aston Villa at home. That was the clincher. The crowd was just under 30,000 and everybody was well keyed-up for it. Villa had a good side. They'd beaten us 3 – 0 just before Christmas so they were no pushover. John Arlott was reporting it that particular day. It was nought – nought at half time and then Crawford got two goals in the second half. Funny thing, the referee was Mr E Crawford of Doncaster.

No one ever thought we'd be champions the first season. They thought we'd do well if we kept in the first division. We're the only side to win it in our first ever season in the first division. That's pretty good going you know! At the end of the game the team did a lap of honour round the ground and the crowd flocked on to the pitch. I just took it as a matter of course. Well, I'd be pleased and I'll give 'em a clap and have a laugh and a talk with someone but that would be it all over. I'm not a singer or a booer, I don't believe in all this shouting and jumping about. I'm like Alf Ramsey. I can sit there without being perturbed, sit there and watch it.

They all reckon Bobby Robson's team of '80 – '81 would've beat them but Ramsey's was a good side you know. Bailey, Carberry, Compton, Nelson, BAXTER, Ellsworthy, Stephenson, Moran, Crawford and Phillips, LEADBETTER, that was a GOOD side. You see, Leadbetter, he converted him from an inside man into a left winger and he had a marvellous season. They only called on 16 players that season. Ken Malcolm played in the first three games, then he had sciatica and John Compton come in and played the rest of the season. Aled Owen played in one game at Christmas when Jimmy Leadbetter was injured. Dermott Curtis played sometimes and Reg Pickett played when Billy Baxter couldn't get army leave. Ray Crawford was leading scorer in the second division in '60 – '61, then top scorer in the first division in '61 – '62, when he got 40 goals. He was a fairly big fella but he had a lot of skill on the ball and he was capped for England that season. He was born on July 13th, 1936, so he'd be 58 now. He had a car, that used to be PPV121. That was a fair good car...it weren't an Austin, might have been a Morris. Roy Bailey used to have a car that was a Standard, ROY558. Then he got rid of that and had a Triumph, LPV2024 I think it was. Few years ago now! Alf Ramsey had a Ford Consul, WNU929. John Ellsworthy used to have his father-in-law's, HOM622, but hardly any of the others had cars then. They used to have bicycles.

John Ellsworthy is still here and I ain't seen Roy Stephenson lately but he had a job around here somewhere. Ted Phillips lives at Colchester, Carberry went back to Liverpool. Compton, I think he's back in London. Reg Pickett and Ray Crawford are back in Portsmouth. Billy Baxter, Doug Moran, the inside right, and Jimmy Leadbetter all went back to Scotland. Andy Nelson was manager of Charlton Athletic for a little while, I think he still lives in London. Bailey went to South Africa, he died not very long ago.

"Well let's go for my brothers. Try September 24th, 1961 and August 5th, 1964. That one should be tricky, being the cricket season. September 24th, '61. Right...that was a Sunday. They went to Everton on the 23rd in the first division. No, wait a minute...we played FULHAM at home and lost 4 – 2. Johnny Haynes played for them, just when he got that £100 a week wage. Phillips and Crawford got one apiece that day. Now... August 5th, 1964. I'll soon do that. We played Spurs on Saturday April 4th, 1964, so if you go through the Saturdays...erm...erm...erm...aah! August 1st was a Saturday, so it must have been a Wednesday.

The greatest forward.
Not so much for the number
but the sheer quality of goals
he scored. Tremendous ball
control could get him from
seemingly impossible
situations into goal scoring
positions.

Pelé

(Edson Arantes do Nascimento)

International Caps	110
World Cup Finals Caps	14
World Cup Finals Goals	12
Goals in Career	1200
Year of Birth	1940

Ray Crawford

League Appearances	476
League Goals	290
International Caps	2
International Goals	1
Year of Birth	1936

The Greatest Forward

RAY CRAWFORD

Centre-forward who made 354 appearances and scored 228 goals in two spells at Ipswich Town. Struck both goals in the legendary Championship clinching 2 – 0 victory against Aston Villa on 28th April 1962.

When we were in Ipswich Eileen used to have her hair done and the young girl in there said, 'When my Dad comes home on a Saturday from watching the Town, if they've won, you can get anything out of him you want, but if they lose, you just don't talk to him for two or three days until he's got over it.'
When you're playing you don't notice how much it affects people. Once you've retired and you get to know people differently, then you realise. I was so wrapped up in playing that I didn't realise.

I turned pro with Portsmouth in 1956, then I went to Ipswich, Wolves, West Brom, then Bill McGarry brought me back to Ipswich, then I went to Charlton, then I went non-League to Kettering, next I went to Colchester, then out to Durban City in South Africa, then I came back and finished at Brighton in November 1973. That was my football career. I still look out for 'em all. I even like to see how Kettering are getting on.

I get a lot of pleasure out of just watching football now. At any level. Last Saturday afternoon I went up the local rec and watched three games up there in the rain. Must have thought I was a lunatic. If a fella scores a goal, even on the rec, if he's got the ball down and shown some decent control or sent somebody the wrong way or brought it inside and put in a good shot and come to that if the goalies done a good save, I'm standing on the touch line there clapping him. I watch it all on the television as well, all the 'Euro' goals on Tuesdays, the Italian on Sundays and I pick up the German football. Can't understand a word they're saying.

I'll talk to anyone about football. My wife says if I stopped talking about it at work I'd be home a lot earlier! I'm just like all football fans, I pick my England side. I could never agree with Graham Taylor. I mean fancy playing Lee Sharpe at left back!

I first saw Ipswich play in September 1958 and I thought they were bloody awful. I mean, Pompey were an established first division side and I was being shipped off to Ipswich who were struggling at the foot of the second division. It was at Orient on a Thursday night. I met the team, said hello, watched the game, terrible. Had a chat with Alf Ramsey about one thing and another and I came straight back to Portsmouth that night. The Portsmouth manager was Freddy Cox, and I said to him, 'No, I don't want to go up there, they're not very good anyway, dreadful side,' and he sort of froze me out. For three or four weeks I didn't get any games or anything until in the end I remember knocking on his door and saying, 'I've changed me mind, I'll go.'

It took them a while to warm to me at Ipswich. Eileen used to go to the games with Betty Pickett, Reg's wife and they had so many arguments with the supporters because nobody liked Reg or me. They used to be moving from one part of the ground to another to find somewhere where they liked us! They liked Tom Garneys. Good player, but he was about 34 or 35. He was a hero there and of course we were the new boys. Fortunately, I was a success. I scored 20 goals in so many games for 'em and we consolidated in the division. Portsmouth got relegated that year.

Sir Alf, he certainly got that place going. It all started to come together in '60 – '61. For two seasons teams didn't know how to handle us because they didn't know the way we played. They didn't know we had Stevo and Jimmy Leadbetter as deep mid-field players, so they had two full backs standing there with no one to mark and nothing to do. Ted Phillips and myself used to make these runs in behind them. They weren't with it in those days, were they? Nowadays, if I'm playing Peterborough this week I send somebody to watch them, don't I? He comes back and it's, 'he does this, he does that, he doesn't come off his line for crosses, blah blah,' everybody knows. But in those days you just went out and played! So we won the second division title and then when we got in the first division they just didn't think we'd be a threat.

We were a very small unfashionable club. We was only on £22 a week! Haynesy was on a hundred at Fulham! A lot of 'em was on fifties and sixties. The dressing rooms were a disgrace. We used to hang our coats and trousers at the windows to stop people looking in! They never even had frosted glass! Little Stevo used to stand on the bench to put his trousers on and one day somebody shouted, 'We can see your bottom!' And the bath! You wouldn't put a dog in that nowadays. Our toilets used to be outside in a tin shed! Jimmy Leadbetter used to leave a fag out there and come half-time he'd have a puff, always had his puff. But we were an attractive side. The quality of our passing for those two years was great.

We never thought we were going to win it. Burnley had all those games in hand. That's probably why we just went out and won our games and, of course, they slipped up, didn't they? On the last day of the season we had to beat Aston Villa to stand a realistic chance and they had a good side, a lot of international players, and if Burnley had won their last two games they'd have pipped us. The atmosphere was a bit tense cos we knew we mustn't lose. If we lost...well...I was obviously tense...but it was never thought about...I don't remember even discussing it. I don't remember Alf ever saying, 'We've got a chance of winning the title. Look, if we win this game we'll be so and so.' He kept the pressure off us, he probably had all

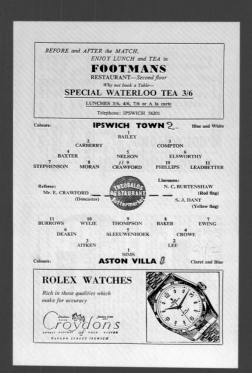

BEFORE and AFTER the MATCH,
ENJOY LUNCH and TEA in

FOOTMANS
RESTAURANT—Second floor
Why not book a Table—
SPECIAL WATERLOO TEA 3/6
LUNCHES 3/6, 4/6, 7/6 or A la carte
Telephone: IPSWICH 56201

Colours: **IPSWICH TOWN 2** Blue and White

1
BAILEY
2 3
CARBERRY COMPTON
4 5 6
BAXTER NELSON ELSWORTHY
7 8 11 9 10 11
STEPHENSON MORAN CRAWFORD PHILLIPS LEADBETTER

Referee: Linesmen:
Mr. E. CRAWFORD N. C. BURTENSHAW
(Doncaster) (Red flag)
S. J. DANT
(Yellow flag)

11 10 9 8 7
BURROWS WYLIE THOMPSON BAKER EWING
6 5 4
DEAKIN SLEEUWENHOEK CROWE
3 2
AITKEN LEE
1
SIMS

Colours: **ASTON VILLA 0** Claret and Blue

ROLEX WATCHES
*Rich in those qualities which
make for accuracy*

Croydons
of GOLD SILVER
TAVERN STREET IPSWICH

the pressure on him. There's a lot of pressure on teams these days. I mean, I read the paper today and Jim Smith said, 'This match against Peterborough is crucial .' We didn't have any of that pressure, Alf didn't say things like that. The build up to the game was exactly the same as always. We never used to get to the ground till quarter past two, they all meet up about mid-day now and have meals together. We got to the ground at normal time, got our complementary tickets, took 'em outside and left 'em on the gate, went in, had a laugh and joke, got changed. Alf came in but he never used to tell us a lot on the day because we had our team talks on the Friday. Everything was really laid back, there was no hype over it at all. We all went out at five to three, I mean nowadays they go out for warm-ups, don't they? We just went out and played. It was a full house and there was a tremendous atmosphere. Lovely sunny afternoon, not too hot. A lovely day for playing football.

We were obviously looking to get the goals, pushing it all the time, but we were nervous and couldn't get the break-through. Derek Dougan was almost playing as an extra centre-half he was that deep. They'd obviously come to defend, but we just stuck at it and although things were getting more and more tense it was just a matter of time. Half-way through the second half, we did it. John Ellsworthy hit the bar and I just followed up. The second one, I was on the half-way line, the ball was played over the top and I went after it, pushed it past the centre-half, just ran and WHACK, had a shot at goal, keeper made the save, it came back to me and I put it in the net from an angle. Once we went two up, we were so on top. There was never any chance that they were going to score. The crowd just wanted us to get more goals. They weren't whistling for time or nothing, they were thoroughly enjoying it. On the day, when we'd actually won, when the Burnley result had come through, it felt great. I think we were all in a bit of shock. The crowd all

came on the pitch and we fought our way through it to get off and then Alf says, 'Go on, get back out! Thank the crowd!' He didn't come out and I don't think Jimmy Leadbetter did either. He was sitting in there having a fag! We went back out and ran round with the crowd but it's all a bit of a haze really. Eventually we came back and got in the bath and Alf said they'd invited us all up to the boardroom for a drink and we'd NEVER, NEVER, EVER been up to the boardroom! And that was it really. I mean we went up there and had a few drinks...and...just went home! I don't remember getting drunk or anything.

I only ever actually won anything at Ipswich, but I had a great time at Colchester United. We were in the fourth division and we drew Leeds in the cup. This was 1972 and they were champions. The whole town was bubbling. People were desperate for tickets, but of course they were in short supply because it's a tiny ground. The manager, Dick Graham, reckoned Gary Sprake was indecisive on crosses so we practised crossing balls in to the edge of that six-yard area. Trained on that all week. On the Saturday, Jack Charlton pushed me over and we got a free kick and it worked out exactly and I scored. Sprakey sort of half came for it and was nowhere. Me and Norman Hunter were walking off together at half-time and he said to me, 'I ducked out of that, thought Gary was coming.' Well he was, but he never got there did he, missed by a mile. Then Brian Gibbs crossed one to the far post and I headed it on to Paul Reaney's back and it was just 'hunt the ball' really. I was on the floor and I just swung me foot and the ball hit the inside of the post and crossed the line. Dave Simmons got a third before they hit us with two goals in ten minutes, but we just held on. When the final whistle went at quarter to five they sprinted off the pitch and they'd left Colchester by five o'clock! They didn't sign autographs for the kids or nothing. They were in that coach and gone!

We were having a great time, we were everywhere, everybody wanted to buy us a drink. That was a great occasion for Colchester. They gave us a civic reception for that.

I can remember all my goals. I was a six yard man. Never used to head the ball hard. I placed my headers, used to go 'dink' and the keeper couldn't get to 'em. I hardly ever used to shoot from outside the box cos I hadn't got a very hard shot but I won a big trophy for 'Goal of the Season' on Anglia Television. They sent it through the post and it arrived broken, so I patched it up best I could. It was a goal I got up at Everton. It was a brilliant move, I can remember it now. It went from keeper, to full back, to midfield, then it was played up to me and I dummied to go one way, went the other and hit it from outside the box.

I remember that match really well cos actually my second goal I punched in the net! Gordon West, their keeper went to grab the ball on the goal line and I just punched it in. I looked round to the linesman and he was gone, the referee was gone, they were both on the half-way line waiting to restart! Everybody else saw it. They were calling me a cowboy and all sorts! That made it 2 – 2, then they got a penalty in the last seconds. Alan Ball hit the post, it came back to him and he whacked it in the net and went charging off thinking he'd scored the winner. Course it wasn't, was it. He was offside, another player's got to play the ball! Boy, I took a lot of abuse from the crowd that day!

Nowadays, soon as they've scored they run to the crowd, as if they've done it all themselves. I always used to think it was the team. The first person you've got to go to is the person who's crossed it or passed it to you. Mind you, give me the ball in the box, I'll never pass it. Probably should have done a lot more than I did, but a striker has to be selfish. I wanted to score every time I played. If we won and I didn't score, I felt I hadn't done my bit. Goals, that's what it was all about.

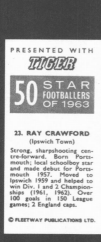

PRESENTED WITH
TIGER

50 STAR FOOTBALLERS OF 1963

23. RAY CRAWFORD
(Ipswich Town)

Strong, sharpshooting centre-forward. Born Portsmouth; local schoolboy star and made debut for Portsmouth 1957. Moved to Ipswich 1959 and helped to win Div. 1 and 2 Championships (1961, 1962). Over 100 goals in 150 League games; 2 England caps.

© FLEETWAY PUBLICATIONS LTD.

The worst thing about football is:

getting up on Sunday morning,
I'm always knackered after the game,
when you ache and you have to hobble home.
When you get a bad foul, *especially on your knees.*
When it's dry and you slide tackle and it burns your legs.
Getting changed in the cold.

I wish it didn't hurt so muc

Then I'd be blinding wouldn't I?

When you lose, but we're used to that.

When you play really well and deserve to win but you lose.
When it's freezing cold. When you're stiff and you start to run and your
ankles hurt and your legs have gone purple and the Ralgex only starts
working when you've finished playing. That's terrible and it starts burning
up when you don't need it any more.
Sometimes it's worse in the summer when your mouth goes all dry and
you've got no spit in there.
When the ball hits your freezing leg.
When they're picking the teams you might be the last person to be picked.
That don't make you feel right good.

every time you headed it.

The best thing about football is:

playing when it's muddy,
it's great when the pitch is waterlogged,
I like the skill involved,
overhead kicks, scoring the winner in the last minute,
I like scoring goals.
It feels great. I can't compare it to anything else.
Scoring a goal just sends a shiver down you for about five seconds.
That's where you get all these daft dances from.
It gets you out of the house to see your mates.
If I didn't play football, I'd have to stay in and do my homework.

It's better than going to church...

I look forward to it, coming down and having a laugh.
You're with your football mates –
You think
roll on Saturday.

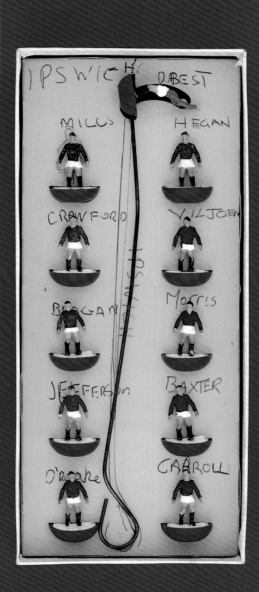

WYN DAVIES
NEWCASTLE UNITED

CENTRE FORWARD

RALPH COATES
BURNLEY

INSIDE RIGHT

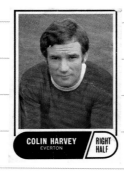

COLIN HARVEY
EVERTON
RIGHT HALF

IAN PORTERFIELD
SUNDERLAND
LEFT HALF

JIMMY GREAVES
TOTTENHAM HOTSPUR
INSIDE RIGHT

BRYAN ROBSON
NEWCASTLE UNITED
INSIDE RIGHT

BOBBY MOORE
WEST HAM UNITED
LEFT HALF

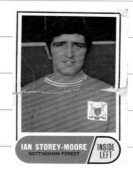

IAN STOREY-MOORE
NOTTINGHAM FOREST
INSIDE LEFT

SAM ELLIS
SHEFFIELD WEDNESDAY

BILL GLAZIER
COVENTRY CITY
GOAL KEEPER

GEORGE MULHALL
SUNDERLAND
OUTSIDE LEFT

PETER HINDLEY
NOTTINGHAM FOREST
RIGHT BACK

JOHN OSBORNE
WEST BROMWICH ALBION
GOAL KEEPER

IAN COLLARD
IPSWICH TOWN
INSIDE RIGHT

JOHN KAYE
WEST BROMWICH ALBION
LEFT HALF

FRANCIS BURNS
MANCHESTER UNITED
RIGHT BACK

JIM McCALLIOG
WOLVERHAMPTON WANDERERS
INSIDE RIGHT

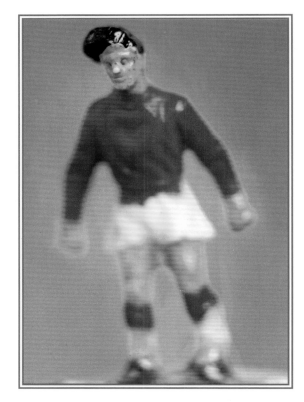

alive & kicking

Alive and Kicking

DR HUGH SIMONS

'I was at a meeting of the Royal Society of Medicine yesterday and they showed graphs which demonstrate how thigh muscles decrease in strength as you get older, right up to your seventies. I'm quite pleased that mine aren't working too badly at 77 years of age. When I went to the sports shop to buy my last pair of boots they said, *'Is it for you, sir?'* They couldn't believe it when I said, *'Yes.'* I've had these boots a few years now. I knock the mud off them every week, that's about enough. I'm not one for doing a big boot clean!

It's just the sheer desire to play. I love football and I want to be out there with the lads. I enjoy the banter in the dressing room and going for a few drinks afterwards. In the old days, before breath tests and so on, there would be many a pint sunk and people used to have quite a party.

I started in Finsbury Park when I was four and I had my second game in Finsbury Park when I was 64. I remember, when I was seven or eight, insisting that my mother should buy me a full-size football. I had to have a full-size ball. Even then I think I had an appreciation of what a beautiful game it is.

I must have been about ten when my father first took me along to see Arsenal. Of course, they were a great team in the Herbert Chapman days, played beautiful attacking football and there were some very fine mid-field players. 'Iron Man' Wilf Copping, Alex James, who was unbelievably clever, and David Jack, who had this 'fluttering' foot. He'd take the ball along and sort of flutter his foot over the ball so the bloke didn't know whether he was going to stop, go on or what, and he had a very fine body swerve. I'm not really so keen on Arsenal these days because I don't like the style of football they play.

Nowadays they don't value skill. Beardsley's had two or three years out of the England team for no reason at all. Old Graham Taylor seemed to have such a low opinion of English football that he thought you could only win by playing what he called the 'English' game, which seemed to me to be 'kick and rush'. And he got worse and worse. I mean, I quite like the chap as a chap, but the extraordinary things he did! He played that international without a left-back! And when Clough was due to go on as substitute, you heard it on the box, he was asking Taylor which side of the field he should play on! Well, I mean that should have been worked out ages before! Poor old Graham Taylor. He should never have been manager of England.

I was captain of my school team and our coach was a chap called Bert White. He taught you how to pass the ball. He was a coach at Wimbledon as well and when I was about 17 he took me off there and I played for the youths, reserves, and I had one or two games for the firsts. He wouldn't have stood for the Wimbledon of recent years. They play some pretty rough stuff and he wouldn't have stood for that. None of those players would have been in his team. Vinny Jones! Out!!

They wanted me to stay on and I really wanted to give it a go but unfortunately I had to give it up. By then, at my father's insistence, I was a medical student over in Paddington. Football was always a stronger draw than doctoring and I was furious because to get your day's work done and then to train was impossible. Possibly, with the extra training and so on, I might have made the pro game, but I've got a feeling I wouldn't have had the physical strength. Anyhow, over the years I played for United Hospitals, Westminster Old Boys and Corinthian Casuals where I had a game or two with Bernard Joy, who'd played for Arsenal, so I played to a pretty high standard.

I once played in an army game out in the Middle East and I found after about 10 minutes that the confounded bloke who was marking me seemed to know exactly what I was going to do, seemed to be able to take the ball away from me as he wished, very strong in the tackle, could do exactly what he liked. I'd never come up against such a good player. I thought, 'this damn fellow is far too good for me,' so I persuaded the captain to put me over the other side of the field and had a much better game in the second half! Afterwards I found out it was Alf Ramsey. He was 23 and a Southampton player at the time. The following year he became an international.

I've had quite a few injuries over the years. The quadruseps and hamstrings in both my legs have gone more than once. I had an achilles tendon injury when I was 64 and I had my jaw broken when I was playing for

Corinth' Casuals against Dulwich Hamlet. They had an international half who'd tuck his hand inside my shorts and pull me back every time there was a throw-in or corner. Then, in the second half I went up to head the ball and this chap came backwards in a most reckless way and hit me across my face with the back of his head, after I'd headed the ball away! I was looking up the field to see where the ball had gone and I got this almighty bang in my face. It was damn painful. Absolutely no need to do that at all! After the pain had worn off a bit I was very angry and I thought, 'I'm going to get this bloke, I'll fix him somehow,' and I waited for my chance.

Well, right near the end there was a mêlée in the goal mouth and I saw this chap was just in front of me and I whipped round and delivered him a smart kick on his ankle, and he went down howling with pain! The referee never saw it! One of our blokes said to me, 'You can't do things like that!' And I said, 'Can't I?' I wouldn't like to try that now, but I was young enough then. Afterwards when I tried to drink a beer I found I couldn't open my mouth properly. I had to have it operated on and they wired up all my teeth. Couldn't eat. All I could do was drink soup and beer and I lost a stone!

I used to see Fulham a lot. That was a nice ground to go to. A very pleasant ground to watch the football from. That was at the time of Bobby Robson, Johnny Haynes, Jimmy Hill and 'Tosh' Chamberlain. Tosh was the Fulham outside-left and he was one of those chaps who had quite a turn of speed and a good left foot but nothing much else. When it came to the finer arts of ball control he wasn't too hot, but he was a pretty useful left winger because he could whip in some good crosses and occasionally hit a cracking good shot.

At that time I was working at St George's on Hyde Park corner and one day I got a phone call from the senior psychiatrist who said, 'I've got a professional footballer here. I don't think there's much wrong with him...you know...mentally. He seems a bit...simple. Can I send him

round to you?' Quarter of an hour later, a familiar figure comes in to my office. It was old Tosh Chamberlain. Then I got a very confused story, but what it boiled down to was that Tosh had totally lost his confidence. He thought the crowd didn't like him, his wife didn't like him and, most important of all, Johnny Haynes didn't like him! Johnny Haynes, who was a great passer of the ball, would get the ball in mid-field and deliver a beautiful pass to Tosh with absolute pinpoint accuracy, but instead of bringing it under control, Tosh would let it bounce off his foot and in to touch. That irritated Johnny considerably and Tosh had got in to a terrible state and things were getting worse and worse. Instead of concentrating on getting in to good positions and keeping an eye on the full-back, he was nervously looking at Johnny all the time so when the ball came his way he was easily dispossessed.

Well, first of all I thought, 'What the hell! Why isn't the manager dealing with this? This isn't really a medical problem.' But apparently Tosh was too frightened to say anything to the manager. So I said, 'Look here, the next time Johnny gets the ball, take a look up the wing, see where the full-back is and as the ball comes across, look as though your going to cut in, then go shooting down the wing. That'll deceive the full-back.'

'Oh,' he said, 'Thanks very much.'

He took it all in. Then he said, 'I can't seem to take a corner nowadays.' So we got a tennis ball on the floor and he and I then shaped up for kicking corners. Here was I showing this first division professional how to kick a corner! And he was saying, 'Thank you very much.'

This was just before Easter and I was going away on a football tour. I remember on the Easter Monday picking up the paper at breakfast, and there in big headlines was CHAMBERLAIN'S GREAT COMEBACK, TOSH GETS 2 AGAINST THE SPURS. Apparently he had a great game!

I went and watched Fulham again a few weeks later and he definitely seemed to have got his confidence back. I don't know whether it improved his marriage as well!

I still turn out for the London Hospital's Sunday side. The games are played in a pretty good spirit and you don't get any nasty tackling really. I've never tired of it, but I have felt that I haven't really been giving enough to the team. Four years ago I said, 'No, this is it lads, I'm finished.' But they rang me up at the beginning of the next season when I wasn't feeling too bad and here I am.

I play on the left-wing and if I get the ball with a bit of time I reckon I can perhaps put in a useful pass and create an opening. My goal scoring is the thing that upsets me. I used to get a few goals but I don't seem to be able to now. Last Sunday I had two reasonable chances and I found the target all right, but I couldn't hit it hard enough. I got one at the end of last season, but that was a penalty which doesn't really count. The season before was the last time I scored in open play. Fortunately, I got the ball with a bit of time and I managed to get inside the box and hit it hard and low inside the near post. When I was younger I got some goals in cup ties which were really quite useful, but I can remember the ones I missed much better because it was invariably something very important. I'd get myself in to these good positions but then there was always the anticipation, 'Ah, yes, a GOAL, at an IMPORTANT TIME.' Then I'd go and miss it!

About mid-week I take a ball out on Streatham Common and for about half an hour I trot about and kick it around, just to get the feel of it. Sometimes of course kids come up and then I'm in real trouble. They can go on for hours! Got in with a fine bunch of chaps once. They must have been the local school First Eleven because the ball was flying about, very good passes coming. At first they thought, 'Old buffer, we'll make fun of him,' but after a time they found that I could pass the ball too.

When I was a boy, if you went out on the local common on a Saturday morning, there were so many people there kicking balls about you had to really fight to get a place.

But now, you go out to Streatham Common on a Saturday morning you'll find you're the only person there. No kids! *Where do they all get to?*

'All I ever wanted to do was play football.'

'I hate it when the ball hits you in the face. Someone did a volley from close in and it hit me face. I was in reet pain.'

When I pull off a really *good save*

I just think...YES!!!!!!!!!!

'When we go down t' field after school we tek corners and do headers _and I_ go in goal. There are full size nets and we're only small lads so you sometimes have to do reet big dives. If you do a dive and miss the ball you hurt yourself but it's really good when you do a reet big dive and tek it down and keep hold of the ball.
I've always dreamed of running out, diving at someone's feet and flying up in the air over them.'

If the mud weren't there you'd see all scars on my legs. When it's P.E. at school they think I get beaten up. 'Now Charlene, I think we should have a chat. Is everything all right at home? Why don't you give it up, you always have these cuts and bruises?' But they don't understand how much I love it. When football crops up in the conversation they go, 'Oh no, not again!'

The Summer of '39

PETER HARVEY

'*I was ten* 10°

and this was

fantastic.

I loved football.

I used to go to all the matches
at Fratton Park,

even at that age.'

... Pompee Play Up!

Play Up Pompeee!

Play Up Pompeee!... Pompee Play Up!

... Pompee Play Up!

Play Up Pompeee!

Play Up Pompeee! ... Pompee Play Up!

Play Up Pompeee!... Pompee Play Up!

Play Up Pompeee!... Pompee Play Up!

There was a lot of excitement in the town when Pompey got to the final in '39. My father had a sort of general drapers shop. It wasn't a big store but it had a men's and ladies department and being a great follower of Portsmouth he decided, more or less as a promotion, to offer a suit to everyone who scored a goal.
He put up a display in the men's department window,
'Harvey's Sporting Offer. A Suit for Every Goal!' He wrote to the club about it and they sent us three tickets to the final, for my father and mother and me.

Play Up Pompeee!... Pompee Play Up!

Play Up Pompeee!

Play Up Pompeee!

The day was great. We decorated the car with ribbons and rosettes and drove up to London. There was no traffic about in those days, so that was easy, and you could park right by the stadium. We didn't expect to win of course because we were fairly well down the bottom of the first division and Wolves were nearly at the top. It was just a question of how many goals the Wolves were going to get! We hoped to win but, well, all the papers were giving it to Wolves.

When Pompey scored the first goal we all went mad! That was in the first half and I think we scored another before half-time. Ooh yes, there was singing! Every time we scored a goal the Pompey chimes rang out...'*Play up Pompee...Pompee play up!*' *Fantastic* atmosphere. There must have been 25,000 there from Pompey. I think we went 3 – 0 up, then Wolves got one and our faces dropped a bit, but Pompey were all over them in the last ten or twelve minutes. They could have had more but they were trying hard to get the right-winger a goal cos he was an older member of the team – Worral, bald-headed chap. Anyway, we did get another one and it finished 4 – 1. Nobody really thought Pompey would win, and to win by such a margin was unbelievable!

I don't think anybody had got four in a Cup Final before, and I don't know whether they have since actually. It was so exciting. To be a boy of ten...I'd have been terribly disappointed if we'd lost. To be on the winning side was wonderful. All the Wolves fans were very dejected.

After the game my father thought his offer was a bit unfair so he gave the rest of the team a blazer and flannels, but suits to the three goal scorers. Parker scored twice so he got two and he gave his other suit to the captain. Anderson got one, then was it Barlow who got the other one? So, in return for doing this the football club allowed my father to have the Cup on show in the shop window for a fortnight, which was probably a risky business even in those days.

He displayed the suits as well, with the player's name on each one. It took off like a bomb! Crowds used to gather outside! If I remember rightly there was always a policeman hovering in the vicinity. People were coming in and saying, *'Can I have a suit like Parker's please? Can I have a suit like Barlow's please?'* Sold endless number of suits!

My father did exceptionally well out of that actually, so I don't suppose it cost him anything to give away the suits in the first place. He'd gone down to Fratton Park and collected the Cup in the car, brought it home, opened up the case, the blue and white ribbons were on it, and I just held it up. I was quite taken aback the first time I held it. I mean, to actually *hold* the F.A. Cup! That was quite something.

He used to take it to work with him in the morning, display it in the window and then at about half-past ten or eleven at night I'd go with him down to the shop. It was a very exciting time! Normally I would have been in bed by eight or half-past! We'd take the Cup out from the window, put it back in its wooden box, put it in the car, take it back home, take it upstairs and put it at the foot of the bed, and that's where it would stay all night. On Sundays it sat on the sideboard, on its very big plinth. I used to stand there and just stare at it. Later on, when things had settled down a bit, we had all the neighbours round and we all had a drop of champagne out of it and I think we took it out in the garden on a table and some photos were taken then.

That one match. You know, if I'd never seen any other, that's the one.

When we were kids it was down to Fratton Park on the trolley bus and in the back entrance. It was about one and nine to get in. I think it was three and six in the seats in the main stand. When I was very young I was always down the front, so my head was probably about the same level as the pitch. I'm not very tall now but it was a bit of a tiptoe job. Sometimes we used to go behind the goal for a change, but I would rather be as near to the centre line as I could get. I can remember how packed it was in the North Stand. You'd walk along that little trough at the back and there would appear to be nowhere to go...there really was nowhere to go! It was full up, chock-a-block! You used to have to wriggle your way in, wriggle your way down as far as you could, *pushing*.

I preferred to stand than to sit. I had sat once or twice when my father took me, but there wasn't the atmosphere sitting with space between you as there was being *packed* in. I don't think they'll ever get the same atmosphere in all-seater stadiums. There was such a jam when we came out. Everybody was squeezed together. We used to pick both feet up of the floor and be carried with the crowd for yards and yards. It was amazing... such a crush.

I've got an idea, I may be wrong, that 46,000 was the biggest gate and it's a reasonably small stadium. When people started to sing they would all *sway* and you looked over opposite and all the whole mass of people, thousands of people, were swaying from side to side, singing their heads off! Unbelievable sight! *'Play Up Pompeee!...Pompee Play Up!...Play Up Pompeee!...Pompee Play Up!'* The famous Pompey chimes! I don't know when it first started but it's stayed with the team all my life. It's to the Westminster chimes. I heard them the Saturday before last when they beat Charlton and I knew Pompey had scored a goal even from this distance, which is a mile and a half, I suppose. I know if they've nearly scored because as they get nearer the goal there's a roar and the noise reaches a crescendo, but then when he misses it goes *AAAaaaahhh*...and the cheer drops away quickly. But when they score a goal, the roar goes on and on and on and then it's immediately followed by the Pompey Chimes.

Whitley Bay Boy's Club 0
Cramlington Juniors 1

"We was robbed".

115

Roy Rovers

121

16A 17 17A

11

GEORGIE

8   18A   19

11

DIVISION ONE

	P	HOME			Goals		AWAY			Goals		
		W	D	L	F	A	W	D	L	F	A	Pts
Ipswich	42	17	2	2	58	28	7	6	8	35	39	56
Burnley	42	14	4	3	57	26	7	7	7	44	41	53
Spurs	42	14	4	3	59	34	7	6	8	29	35	52
Everton	42	17	2	2	64	21	3	9	9	24	33	51
Sheff. U.	42	13	5	3	37	23	6	4	11	24	46	47
Sheff. W.	42	14	4	3	47	23	6	2	13	25	35	46
Aston V.	42	13	5	3	45	20	5	3	13	20	36	44
W. Ham	42	11	6	4	49	37	6	4	11	27	45	44
W.B.A.	42	10	7	4	50	23	5	6	10	33	44	43
Arsenal	42	9	6	6	39	31	7	5	9	32	41	43
Bolton	42	11	7	3	35	22	5	3	13	27	44	42
Man. C.	42	11	3	7	46	38	6	4	11	32	43	41
Blackpl.	42	10	4	7	41	30	5	7	9	29	45	41
Leics.	42	12	2	7	38	27	5	4	12	34	44	40
Man. U.	42	10	3	8	44	31	5	6	10	28	44	39
Blackbn.	42	10	6	5	33	22	4	5	12	17	36	39
Brnghm.	42	9	6	6	37	35	5	4	12	28	46	38
Wolves	42	8	7	6	38	34	5	3	13	35	52	36
Not. F.	42	12	4	5	39	23	1	6	14	24	56	36
Fulham	42	8	3	10	38	34	5	4	12	28	40	33
Cardiff	42	6	9	6	30	33	3	5	13	20	48	32
Chelsea	42	7	7	7	34	29	2	3	16	29	65	28

'I remember the 1966 World Cup at Wembley.

We lived across from the Red Rum pub at the time.

When England scored I went running out the house into the street, arms up in the air cheering, and all the kids all the way down the street were cheering. When Germany scored we'd all run out and go, 'booo', giving a thumbs down.

It were great.

I was nine years old then.

When he cracked the fourth in everybody was out, mums, dads and all!'

He was a character was Harry you know.
They used to say,

'Him in the red

and white house

why yes Harry Hutchinson, we know him.' He was well known.

Our house was on wheels on a Saturday morning. I got everything out ready for him. Red and white shirt, red and white socks, he virtually had a uniform he used to wear and you know he had a scarf, it was filthy! And would he let me wash it? *'You're not washing that,'* he says, *'It'd be unlucky!'*

Why he wore it and wore it...
Actually, I draped it over the coffin
when he was buried.

He wouldn't He wouldn't part with that scarf.

SUNDERLAND

The women I used to know, their husbands weren't really football supporters, not like Harry. And they used to say, *'I don't know how on earth you live with him. How do you put up with it? Out all hours like that and never knowing where he's at! Vera, if he was mine I would do this and do the other...'* But I just says, *'Why it's his life.'*

I met Harry in 1953. Let me think, I would've been about 23, and he was about seven year older than me. We met in Durham Library actually and we just got on talking an' that. Before I started going out with him serious, I heard about how mad he was on football and how he'd never let anybody get in the way of football. It was well known, you see. Everybody knew Harry. They used to say, *'If you can get him to the altar you must be some woman!'*

When he proposed to me he said, 'Mind the condition, you don't stop me from going to football matches. I must have Saturdays for the football.' And I still said yes. I must have been mad. We even got married on a Wednesday because of the match he wanted to see on the Saturday...Aston Villa I think it was. It was a very quiet wedding, well, there was about thirty people there. We would have had more if it'd been a Saturday. I sometimes wonder why I did it, but I did. We only had a couple of days away in Scarborough and then we had to be home at 12 o'clock and he left me at me mother's and dashed off to the match. Then he used to disappear every Saturday and I just sort of fell in with it really. I thought, *'Will he mellow with age?'* But Harry got worse as he got older. I used to say, *'Why, you might get old and won't get to the matches in the cold and the damp an' that,'* but he liked it. The colder and the wetter it was the more he liked it!

He knew every nook and cranny down at Roker Park. I mean he'd gone from being a boy of about seven year old. His father took him to his first game. When he was a young lad he got in all ways without paying, you know how kids do. He made me laugh, he said, 'I once followed the pie man in selling pies!'

'Ee,' I says, *'You'll do anything you, for football.'*

Let's see, he started decorating the house in about 1970. He had everything red and white. Anything he could lay his hands on. He just suddenly started painting bits. He had red and white paper on the chimney breast, red and white tiles on the kitchen floor, but I liked them meself, and then it went from that on to something else and on to something else. I mean you canna live with red and white all the time, can you? It was a bit far fetched and it would have gone further if he'd only had himself to please.

When they won the Cup at Sunderland – was it 1973? – he was going to do the lawn! I says mind, *'I'm drawing the line there, you're not doing that!'* But he had a great big banner and flags out in the front garden. People used to walk round here, just to see what he was doing. Mad. Absolutely mad. Oh, the night before he went to Wembley he was impossible. I says, *'You should have gone to the doctor's and asked him to calm you down.'* And he was just laughing about it and says, 'I'm calm enough.'

Ee, he was proud when they won. He came home about 5 o'clock in the morning drunk. He had a little cup, like, that he'd bought and he brought me back a red and white ribbon so I'd know Sunderland had won. And he was running down the street with his red and white hat on, on top of his other hat. I says *'Everybody will know you're here, you!'* And he couldn't settle. I've never known him be so excited. No sooner was he in than he was out round the village again. When the men got moving about, you know buying the papers and that, ee, he was out all the morning telling them all about Wembley. He was so excited I said, *'You'll have to have a tranquilliser if you don't give over!'* And would you believe it he watched it right through again on television? That was when they scored one goal, wasn't it? Yes, Leeds wasn't it? I mean he really enjoyed that!

When I came out of hospital after I'd had Shirley, I think he must have been up all night getting things just so because he knew I would've gone mad. He'd left everything in the house ready but when I came out he'd gone! Disappeared! To the match! Not many men would do that the first day of coming home would they? And to crown it all he'd got the wrong milk! He'd got the wrong strength milk for a new baby, so me brother-in-law had to get the car out and go and get some fresh, you know,

decent baby food. Well I just accepted it. It was a Saturday. I thought, *'Oh, he wants to go to the match.'*

She was born on the Thursday so that saved that! I don't know what he would have done if she'd been born on a Saturday. I used to say, *'If I collapsed at your feet you'd never know. You'd step over me and go to a match!'*

You know he called her Shirley because he was a great fan of Charley Hurley. He said, **'We'll put an *S* in front of Hurley and make a Shirley.'**

She used to say,

'Mam, me dad's not right!'

He did spend a fortune on football. We could have bought a house over and over. He made money from his work an' that, but it nearly all went on football and the last time he bought a season ticket I bought it for him. It was over a hundred pound, I think, then. He didn't have the money! But he says, 'They'll go! After this week I'll not get the chance!' I was always going to get it back but I never did. When they went to Wembley in 1973 they couldn't get tickets through supporters clubs then and ooh, he paid ever so much over the top for his ticket and I never got to know to this day what he paid for it. I says, *'How much did you pay for that?'* 'I'm not telling you cos there'll just be a row so don't ask!'

Ee, I could have been sittin' here in a house with grounds and everything if I'd never let him go.

I did go to the home matches a bit later on, when our Shirley was old enough to be left. For about three year I went to all the home matches. He had his own routine, Harry, he got off to the match and he always used to park in the same place, the **'lucky spot'**. Then we'd walk down and go in two betting shops. He liked a bet. Then he used to get down to the ground and he went to the office when he got there cos he knew everybody you know, all the top ones an' that and he used to have a chat and by the time that was over we used to get into our seats. And then the match started.

If I didn't come back with a black eye I nearly did because he was up and down, you know, and his elbows was flying, his arms was flying. He once threw a good hat on the field he was that excited. We never got it back! I used to be busy telling him to be quiet, I used to say *'Everybody's listening to you. Be quiet!'* But he was shouting, 'Take the dirty bugger off!' Going on like that all the time. Or, 'What a bloody fool! Get 'im off!' He was never still for a minute. I enjoyed it, but I never understood a lot of it. I used to keep asking of him and he used to get vexed. 'All this time and you can't understand that! Don't ask such daft questions. Just watch that goal there. If the ball goes in we've scored!' In those days, when Harry went without me he used to stand on the – what-you-call? – the terraces, and I once went with him. He used to know everybody there. He loved it. The Clock Stand they used to call it. The Clock Stand.

For the long trips to away games, I used to get up at about half-past three in the morning and cook him breakfast. There's not many who would've done that. I used to say, *'This must be a labour of love or else I would never do it!'* And I've seen him go out the door at four in the morning and it's been bleaching with snow an' wet and he's gone through that. And if they played a long distance during the week, on a Tuesday night it usually was, they used to drop him off at Durham on the way back and he'd walk home from there at three o'clock in the morning, hail, rain or snow. Hey, he's put some work into Sunderland Football Club!

When he got back late, after 12 o'clock at night, I used to go to bed and if they won I could hear him coming up the stairs, **'By! What a bloody goal! It wasn't half good!'** And then if they didn't win, 'They give it away! They didn't even try, the daft buggers!' And many's the time he'd wake up in the morning saying he'd dreamt he'd scored some goal or something. I used to make-believe I was asleep because I didn't want to hear about it. He talked to us anyway! I mean he wanted somebody to talk about it with. That's why he used to get in the garden on a Sunday morning! Everybody that passed used to come over to him and talk about the match. I says, *'Well you don't do much gardening!'*

Everything he did seemed to revolve around football. He hated the summer, used to count it off the calender, used to say, 'Another so many days and three o'clock and it'll be kick-off!'

The only time he missed a game was when my daughter was married. They were playing at Portsmouth and I said, *'You canna go that day!'* And he was ringing up to Portsmouth every half hour. It cost him a fortune to see who was winning an' that. He'd say, 'Oh I wish that service was over and I could get back and see what they're doing, the kick-off will be on now down there!' I says, *'Ee, I don't know how you dare! In church!'* But he says, 'Why the first goal might have gone in.' And they was laughing at him at Hogarth Manor where we had the reception.

He once went with a broken foot. He broke his ankle and he had it in plaster and when the Saturday came I said *'You can not go to the match.'* They were playing at home and he says, 'I'm gonna try!' And I went out to do some shopping and when I came back the house was

empty. He'd gone. He hobbled down to that match, stood on his good leg and it took the cramp. In the end they had to get him into a taxi to get him home! Mind, I nearly walked out on him that time.

I did get sick of it. It interfered with everything. I couldn't plan to do anything. There's many a time been about eight or nine people in our kitchen asking him questions. He was telling them all about football. He talked and talked for hours. 'That was the year so and so...' and he used to tell all about who scored. '...Well Mr Hutchinson who did that?' And then he'd start off another story. Ee, I hit the roof...'Why?' he says, 'They were asking questions and I was just telling them.'

When we went out I used to say, 'And don't start with football!' But we no sooner got into a place and they used to come over. 'Well Harry, what did you think today?' And he was off again! I used to say, 'You're worse than the children to go on like that.' He was like a schoolboy. 'I'll be a schoolboy! I'm going to stop this way and all!' You just couldn't vex him about it. He was totally dedicated and he wouldn't, he wouldn't give in to anything! I must have been silly because I used to sit about an hour on me own while he was arguing the toss about football over at the other end of the room! He'd send a drink over and all right, he saw I had plenty to drink, but he used to get carried away, forgot I was there.

Out of all the football fans right up and down the country, he won 'A Fan in a Million'. I was proud of him that day! We went to the Café Royal in London and had a lovely time. He spoke on the stage in front of Frank

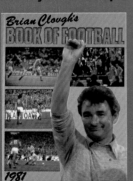

Bough and Brian Clough and all these top people. He was really good and he got a good clap. He spoke about things I never knew and I thought, 'Why, he is interesting when he starts.' Trevor Brooking was there. Can you remember him? And we sat at a table with Bobby Robson and of course he's from this area and he says, 'Well, I'm pleased to meet you Harry!' He made such a fuss of him! Harry was over the moon.

We once went to lunch with Brian Clough an' all, you know. His son was with him, the one called...Nigel.

By, he was a little sod! Ee, he wouldn't behave himself. I says, 'If I had him, I'd give him such a good clout!' Running in and out, banging doors an' that and he took no notice of anybody at all. Ee, he was a bad little boy. Brian Clough told him to stop but he didn't take any notice, but there again, they were busy talking about football. Harry got on well with him, mind.

He won another thing to go round with 'Match of the Day', you know the T.V. recording of the football matches. The fella in the van was saying, 'We'll make it Trevor Francis's day.' So they'd keep putting the cameras on him. I says to Harry, **'Who's Trevor Francis?'** He says, 'Don't ask them that in there!' And the fella says to me, 'Would you like to have a go? Have a look through there and you'll see the match.' I got focussed on a man eating a pie! Harry says, 'That's typical!' But it was really good that day.

They didn't half look after us.

About three months before he died, when he had his operation, he came out on the Thursday and went to a match on the Saturday. He'd just got the stitches out and he went! I was so worked up about it I even went and got the man next door and says, *'Can you come and talk some sense into him?'* He came in but Harry was taking no notice, and when he went out to that match I thought, *'Well, you'll never come back.'* He looked terrible. That was the last one he went to, like, and ee, he should never have been. He came back and wasn't feeling very well and had to go straight to bed. That's when I could have murdered him.

He always said, 'When I go, don't bother about anything. Just scatter me down Roker Park.' So about four days after the funeral we went down there and all the players stood side by side and a friend scattered his ashes in the goal mouth at the end where he used to sit. It was very sad. He looked up at Harry's seat and he says, *'I can see you sittin' there now. You're watching, aren't you Harry?'* It was lovely the way it was done.

It was all football, even till the day he died. Football. When he was in bed and he was very ill he turned to me one day and he says, 'There's not many that would have put up with what I put you through.' He realised you know...but still, it was him. I couldn't do anything about it could I?

I don't think I would have changed him. No, I don't think so. I wish he was still here doing it. I mean he was on television once or twice, but he was!

They used to say, *'The man with the*

red and white eyes.'

There are 50 super 3D Star Cards to collect

PLAYER **SUPER MAC** CLUB **NEWCASTLE UNITE**

In this book there are 20 spaces for your own gallery of soccer stars in astonishing, life-like 3D. There are more spaces on pages 20, 28, 42, 43, 44, 58, 59, 66 & 67.

You can choose from the complete collection of 50 of these full-colour 3D photographs, which are available only through The Sun.

For each 3D Starcard you want, you must save one Starcard token from The Sun (one or more is printed in The Sun almost ever day); if you want five Starcards, for example you must save five Sun Starcard tokens.

The postcard-size 3D Starcards can be purchased singly, or in lots of 5 or 10. You may buy one, or as many as you like, selecting from the list of available Starcards which wil appear regularly in The Sun.

Each Sun 3D Starcard is an amazingly life-

Make your own 3D soccer star gallery

PLAYER **Bobby MOORE** CLUB **WEST HAM UTD**

...ke full-colour portrait of a soccer star;
...othing like them has been seen in this
...ountry before.

...o help you begin your collection, turn to
...age 98 of this book for your bonus Starcard
...oken. Then complete your unique 3D
...allery of soccer stars by saving the tokens
...rom The Sun — Britain's brightest, liveliest
...aily newspaper!

'I've always *been a magpie,* I've always *collected,*

Programmes of course,

ticket stubs,
rosettes,
badges,
newspaper cuttings,

A N Y T H I N G !

DIXIE DEAN

When you're a kid you've got an insatiable appetite, you start looking for the comics that have got football in and every birthday and Christmas your presents are very simple because as long as it's got a football on it, it's acceptable. So you want your first football and your first pair of boots and all the regalia. Fortunately for my parents clubs didn't change their strips three times a season in those days.

You've got to collect autographs haven't you? I look at my old autograph book now and I think, 'Oh God! It's so sad.' It's all in pencil and smeared, just typical. It's this insatiable appetite to get everything. I guess I was seven when I first went to Margate football club and I've been a lifelong supporter ever since. At first you get your own team's programmes, then programmes of all the Football League clubs, then all the Scottish ones, then the Irish and Welsh. Then you go on to the European ones, the Internationals and then the World Cups. I've now got in excess of 50,000 football programmes, and you think to yourself...Jesus!

It really is an addiction. I can't stop. I can't stop because where do you cut anything like that off? I've got nearly 10,000 books on football. I start getting the club histories. They bring one out on Wrexham and I get it but

I'm not even interested in Wrexham! Where do you stop? I really can't quantify it. I've got hundreds of shirts, hundreds of caps, I just don't know. I don't know anything exactly. I don't have a record where I tick things off. One of my greatest pleasures is to go into my study and open a box and say 'Good Lord, I didn't know I had that!'

My family gets quite distressed at times. We're on holiday together and there I am, diving into second-hand shops and flea markets, anywhere, in all parts of the world, hoping to find some little bit of football. People don't understand and I don't think I can explain it anyhow. Collecting is about the power of possession. It has nothing to do with monetary value.

I met Graham and John at auctions. Pooled together we cover a lot of different areas. The only area where we are weak is works of art. By that I mean quality oil paintings, ceramics, early glass and bronzes. Other than that we're looking out for early shin guards, the ones that were worn outside the socks like breeches in the early 1870s.

We want to create a National Football Museum. Our collection should be available to every football supporter, so they have access to what is rightfully theirs. Of the thousands of people who go to Wembley every year for the F.A. Cup final, how many actually get the opportunity to have a good look at the cup? How many have actually seen a winner's or loser's medal? There are clubs now who when they win one of these trophies actually charge their supporters for a photograph of them holding the cup! It's a scandal in my opinion. Football has taken so much from so many and it's given so little back, especially to the supporters.

If you go into the majority of boardrooms and say, 'Do you know, there's a supporter here today for his one thousandth game following the team,' they don't understand. They don't even care. It's total arrogance. They don't appreciate how much of the heart of a person goes into supporting. There's something in our genes that makes us football fans.

The most I've ever paid is just
under ten thousand pounds for
Dixie Dean's championship
winning medal, the year he
scored sixty goals for Everton.

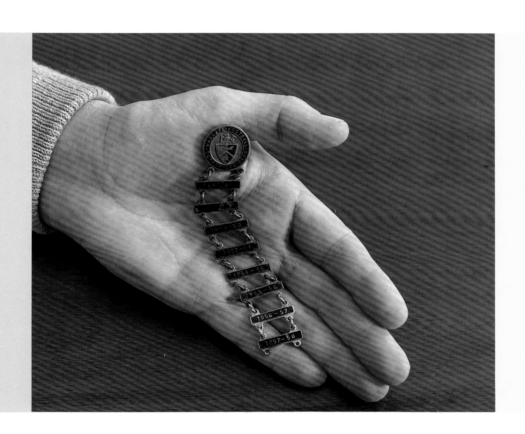

But my first Margate supporters club badge, which has little bars on it with each year written in means just as much to me. I was banned from wearing it at school which I thought was diabolical. **"**

Notes on the archival press pictures.

The majority of the archival press photographs shown here were taken before the 35mm camera, motor drives and powerful telephoto lenses became commonly used. Until the mid-fifties the vast majority of football photographers relied on cumbersome large format press cameras which were aimed in the general direction of the penalty area, the shutters released to capture a goal mouth scramble or a goalkeepers spectacular dive. They exposed on average, a mere six or eight plates during the entire 90 minutes, but the standard, close-up football picture, with which we are all familiar today (telephoto close-ups portraying a clutter of limbs in mid-field), was routinely achieved through ruthlessly cropping from the large format negative. Cropped, these archival prints from thirty or forty years ago are neither better, nor worse, than the hundreds of pictures that are taken at every big match today by photographers with auto-winds. In fact, they are essentially the same. Printed full frame, however, the 5 x 4 images are transformed as, literally, a wider picture is unveiled. We are no longer dealing with conventional football photographs - details - but with beautiful, sweeping landscapes. We are presented with the broader context that includes the crowd, the stadium and a more general view of the match, within which a 'decisive moment' of action is captured. These elements, when combined successfully, relate to the experience of really 'being there' at a game and convey the atmosphere and drama of the occasion.

A message to fact freaks:
You may well discover factual errors within these pages.

Hedley Fairweather

Matthew Fairweather

Hedley Fairweather

Andrea Fairweather

I am, I think my dear lady wife would say, a football fanatic. I think I'd crack up if I didn't have a game. That's the one thing I look forward to at the end of every week. I think, if I get this week over I'm going to, say, Birmingham, on Saturday. It's a drug. I need my fix on a Saturday. The match against Watford was postponed, then the match against Millwall, so I thought, come on, I'll go to Huddersfield. I'll drive anywhere to get to a game: Rochdale, York, Scunthorpe, anywhere.

I think, in order to enjoy football to its full extent you've got to support a team *and* you've got to watch your team. You've got to stick by them, as well, through relegation or whatever. You've got to really love that team.

I'm 50 in four weeks time and I tell you, when we score, I jump up and down as daft as any six year old. I am so pleased. And if we lose, I don't exactly not have any tea, but I don't buy a Sunday paper. What an immense relief at places like Bromsgrove this season. Third round of the cup, we're 1-0 down with two minutes to go, yet we win 2-1. I was giving some of our players some abuse. How fantastically your emotions change. From the pits, from the depths of despair to the height of elation within two minutes, but it doesn't do the old ticker much good. To get two goals!
I couldn't believe it.

That's the true fan, isn't it? Fan comes from the word Fanatic, so it's not a well reasoned thing, is it?